A COMPLETE BEGINNER'S GUIDE TO SERVICED ACCOMMODATION

By

RAY SURGEON

PREFACE

I would like to dedicate this book to my business partner, life partner, personal coach, therapist and best friend Monica. You are the reason we made the venture into property to begin with and I enjoy every day of our lives together.

I would also like to dedicate this book to my mother Gerry who has never really known our struggles and victories with our property venture but who provided the money for our first deposit and sadly recently passed away from a brain tumour. Your strength and sense of humour in the face of everything that life had to throw at you was inspirational and I am lucky to be your son.

My personal Serviced Accommodation journey I would say is still in its early stages, but I feel that I have learned so much in that short space of time and myself and Monica have paid around £14,000 or so on our property education across 2 or 3 years now from different providers teaching different things and I am yet to find a book that details the very essentials of everything from finding the right property to listing your property and start bringing in the cash.

This book marks the start of a property book series where the goal is to give the general property novice enough of the details to get started, without having to shell out anywhere near as much money as we have had to, and something that can be read in one day.

Myself and Monica so far own or control around £1m worth of property, which is a mixture of buy-to-let properties and serviced accommodation units and almost all of that has come about in the past 12 months or so at the time of writing.

As a final disclosure, it has to be mentioned that this book should not be regarded in anyway as any kind of investment advice, we are not FCA regulated and will not be held liable for any losses (financial or otherwise) from any investor using this book as a basis for property investment. I should also say that any views mentioned in this book are the sole views of the author and not necessarily the views of any other person or business.

I would like to thank you very much for purchasing this book and I really hope you find it useful and helps you in your property journey.

INTRODUCTION

I would like to welcome you to the world of serviced accommodation (sometimes referred to as SA). This is the property strategy that by far brings in the most revenue per unit per month but also comes with the most bills and potentially the biggest headaches.

This book aims to educate you on the concept of serviced accommodation, the benefits and most importantly, the risks with this strategy. We will also go through everything on how to secure the property, what type of furnishing and amenities guests expect, the marketing, the cleaning and bed linen changeovers, procedures for check-in, setting your price, getting your property online through the different Online Travel Agents (OTAs), getting paid and dealing with maintenance and guests issues.

So I think the first thing we should clear up is what exactly serviced accommodation is. Serviced accommodation is basically short-term property rentals. The most mainstream example of this is running an AirBnB. It's like running a mini-hotel from a single property.

Serviced accommodation can take different forms, but I would say the most common type of property is an apartment. This is because the majority of guests are either a couple or a contractor coming to an area for a short period of time and would like the privacy and security of a full home, which is close to where they want to visit and is large enough to be comfortable.

One important question to ask would be: Why would someone stay in a serviced accommodation instead of a hotel?

Well, hotels have one major flaw: the rooms are basically an en-suite bedroom and that's it. Serviced accommodation will usually come with a private or shared fully fitted kitchen and when you stay in an area for a week or 2, it gets very expensive to eat out for every meal. This is where S can turn an expensive holiday to an affordable one, especially for families.

Our standard SA is a 2-bedroom flat. This is because the vast majority of providers offer a 1-bedroom flat, which (with a sofa bed) can only fit a maximum of 4 people. This doesn't leave many options for a large family or group of adults. Therefore, we decided to go for the 2 bedroom apartments which can offer up to 6 people and will provide free parking if possible as this can be especially important for contractors and professionals staying in the city for work.

IS SERVICED ACCOMMODATION RIGHT FOR YOU?

I think the first thing to consider is whether or not SA is a good strategy for you. In this section, we will go through the different aspects of serviced accommodation and then maybe at the end you will make a decision as to whether or not you'd be open to taking the plunge of running a serviced accommodation business.

I would say that there are a few things that you should enjoy doing if you are to enjoy operating a serviced accommodation business, including:

- Offering excellent guest experiences
- Speaking to people
- Solving logistical problems
- Furnishing new properties
- Understanding and finding solutions for immediate problems

TIME REQUIRED

One of the most important things to consider especially when starting out is the time that running an SA business takes. This of course depends entirely on the number of units you have, but even a relatively few number of units (say for example, 2 or 3 apartments) can become difficult to manage for 1 or 2 people when you are doing everything yourself.

The most time consuming tasks will be communicating with guests and arranging the changeovers with your cleaners. These need to be performed on a daily and weekly basis.

Now, there are systems you can put in place to deal with all of this guest communication and arrangement with the cleaners but these obviously come at a cost. You will either need to hire someone (which you can do relatively cheaply, hiring a PA from the Philippines at $3 a day for example) but these only work certain hours and with some OTAs you get rated as a host for your responsiveness. You can also set up automatic replies to guests' enquiries, like for example if a guest wants to check-in at a time that's already in your check-in window, their enquiry or request is automatically confirmed.

There are also property management systems such as Tokeet, which will send automatic email confirmations and text messages to your guests, synchronise your calendars across the different OTAs and also manage your pricing but as this is still a relatively small market and burgeoning business, this technology in my experience has been glitchy at best.

There are also SA management companies who will perform all of these activities for you. They will manage the unit for you with the only catch being that most of these companies will charge around 15-20% of your income then you will still obviously have all of the other bills and maintenance to pay for.

So if you're currently working full-time you will need to put as many systems in place as possible to take this load off of you which will cost you more but at least you will be making money and your business will be off the ground.

THIS IS A BUSINESS

One important thing to note is that SA is a business, and needs to be ran as a business. Your properties need constant maintenance and keeping an eye on your monthly expenses is vital. Many people who are familiar with the property industry are very comfortable with the standard buy-to-let model of buying a property, performing some refurbishment and then renting them out for the long term.

In that business model, as soon as the property is let, if you have it managed by a letting agent, you can basically forget about it as long as the tenant pays their rent every month you can forget it and focus your time on other things. This is not the case in serviced accommodation.

The benefit of SA though, is that a property that is usually worth £850 per calendar month as a standard buy-to-let flat can be worth £3,500 per month as a serviced apartment.

RESEARCH

Doing your research and your due diligence is the most important step in assessing any property for any strategy. I hear about so many deals which have put the buyer in trouble because they didn't do the right research on the property. I would say this is even more important when it comes to operating SA, although owners have the back-up plan of just renting it out as a standard buy-to-let if things are going very pear shaped.

In this section we will be going through the core fundamentals of research that simply need to happen before progressing with any property you are considering operating as an SA.

The key question you should be asking in your research is, 'What do I need, to offer a premium product?' and a premium product in SA, is a place that people really want to stay and are willing to pay a higher than average price in order to stay there.

FINDING YOUR AREA

There are a few key factors in determining the area you are going to operate in. The most important of which is the price. I would say that if you have less than £10,000 to invest, then forget about buying a place, you will need to rent. As a rule of thumb, the less money you have to start with, the further North in the UK you will have to go to secure a property.

I think a good exercise would be to have a look at where you are based and think of the surrounding area. Try to think of tourist hotspots or business hub cities like Manchester or Milton Keynes. You are looking for an area which has a relatively large number of people regularly visiting an area within an hours' travel of where you are based, where you can afford to buy or rent a place.

CITY ATTRACTIONS

When you have an idea of the area you think is suitable for a successful SA, a very useful exercise is to try to find out exactly why people would come to visit that area. Is it a tourist hotspot? Is the area known for its nightlife? Is there nothing in the area except for loads of glass office buildings and taxi ranks? This will give you an insight into not only what type of guests are likely to stay in the area, but also gives you an idea of what your marketing will need to be in order to get those guests coming in regularly.

LOCAL CONSTRAINTS

One thing that will definitely require a bit of investigation is the local constraints of the area you wish to operate. One example of this is in London, where any residence used as an SA can only operate as such for a maximum of 90 days in any calendar year. This is known as the '90-day rule'. This is an example of the local council implementing a policy to stop people renting out their property as an SA and you will have to check your local council to see if there are any regulations prohibiting this use. Some councils will also insist on licensing depending on the type of property.

As with all things there are ways around these restrictions. This would be by changing the use from residential to commercial. The one thing to remember in future is that with any kind of rule implementation targeting SA units will only comply to residential properties. This is because hotels are commercial properties and the local councils are very unlikely to implement anything to seriously hinder the hotel industry, so by changing the use you will get around any local council restrictions.

As with everything though, there is always a catch. Switching to commercial use opens up the property to business rates instead of council tax and this can be more expensive (or in some cases, catastrophically expensive) and will require a valuation from the council. For your first property though, you can be entitled to a business rate relief, where if the property is valued under a certain amount, you can be exempt from any business rates.

LOCATION, LOCATION, LOCATION

Once you have an area that ticks all the right boxes, then it's important to really get to know that area and find out the streets where people prefer to stay and also where they would rather not stay.

The simple exercise for this is to log onto Booking.com and search in your selected area and start browsing the properties and hotels available and have a look at the ratings that people have given properties for their location. There is a map function on the search on Booking.com so you can really pinpoint the streets where people like to stay. This is possibly the best indicator of what works and what doesn't because people tell you in their reviews not only where they'd like to stay, but also what they want in the places where they do stay.

AVERAGE NIGHTLY RATES

One key thing that you'll need to figure out is the average nightly rates of the other operators in the area.

If you haven't decided what type of property you'll be targeting yet, then it will be helpful to know the average nightly rates for the weekend (Fri and Sat) and weekday nights (Sun-Thurs) but also find when a big event is happening in the area (like for example a concert or big business event) and see what others are charging on a peak date. This will be for properties that are rated at least 9.0/10 on Booking.com or 4.5/5 on AirBnB, these should be your aim. There is simply much more money to be made when you can offer a premium product.

You will need these average nightly rates for:
- 1-bed apartments
- 2-bed apartments

- 2-bed houses

These properties are offered as a whole and houses which are 3-bed and above are usually offered on a 'per room' basis. It would also be beneficial to get an idea of the prices of hotels in the area and what those hotels can offer. Once you have the average nightly rates for these types of properties, then you'll have a good idea of how much you can charge per night.

OCCUPANCY RATES AND DEMAND

After finding out exactly how much you can charge per night for your potential property, next you will need to find out your average occupancy rate.

There are a few ways of finding this out. If you find a similar property to one which you are thinking of investing in, then have a look at their calendar on AirBnB, you will see how many nights are booked for that month as shown in *Image 1*.

This is to be taken with a pinch of salt because the host can block out dates for many reasons and not just for bookings (like for example maintenance or they may only allow stays on certain days), but if you do this for 3 or 4 properties within your area, this can be a rough indication of the occupancy rate you can expect.

←	September 2018	→

Mo	Tu	We	Th	Fr	Sa	Su
					1	2
3	4	5	6	7	8	9
10	11	12	13	14	15	16
17	18	19	20	21	22	23
24	25	26	27	28	29	30

Updated 13 days ago

Image 1

Another way of assessing demand in the area is by going to Booking.com and performing a search in your area for any particular weekend in the near future and you will hopefully see a message at the top of the search results something similar to *Image 2*.

Image 2

This was a search performed for 2 adults in the Chester area on a weekend in September. Out of 84 apartments, only 6 apartments were available, showing very good demand in that area for apartments. Do this for a couple of dates and make a note of the percentage reserved each time and you will have a good idea for the demand in that area.

ASSESSING YOUR COMPETITION

Another part of your research should be assessing your potential competitors in those areas where guests really want to stay. In particular you should take note of the interior décor, furniture, number of guests and anything that they offer as part of the stay. In some highly competitive areas, hosts will sometimes offer a free bottle of wine or fresh milk and croissants for guests during their stay.

You will need to make a note of anything like this as these are things you are likely to have to offer to get those 9.0/10.0 or 5* reviews from your guests.

You should also have a really good read of the reviews that guests have left as they normally tell you what they love about the property but also areas where you could do better than them.

RESEARCH CONCLUSION

The questions you will need to answer in order to give your SA the maximum chance of success will include:

- Where exactly do guests like to stay?
- What exactly does a premium SA product look like?
- What price are guests happy to pay for a premium product?

- What do guests need so that they will leave a 9.0/10 or 5* review?

When you have very specific answers to these questions above, you will have a very good idea what your SA should look like.

Once you have all this, you should then take that next step and begin the calculations of how much you can make per month from your average nightly rates at average occupancy. The answer to this will give you the answer to whether SA in your chosen area is worthwhile or not. If the average nightly rates are £25, offering free breakfast and in an area where a 2-bedroom flat is around £350,000 or £1,400 per month by renting then it might not be worth your while running your SA business there.

SECURING THE PROPERTY

In this section we will go through the basics of securing the property that you intend to use as an SA. It's important to know what you can do from the outset so that you can properly plan your strategy for maximum success. This, I believe, means creating a formal business plan.

Taking the time to create a business plan does two things: it allows you to set your ambitions properly and also crystallise a pathway to achieve them. As a third benefit, to anyone you may approach for funding, this shows you are serious and have taken the time to seriously consider how your business would run and the profitability of it.

Ultimately, securing any property will come down to either buying or renting the property. This would obviously depend on your capital available from the beginning, but there are positives and negatives for both strategies, both of which we'll go through in this section.

BUYING

If you are in the enviable position of being able to buy the property you're looking to use as SA, then there are multiple considerations in what concerns a purchase that you need to be aware of, that are specific to this use of property and don't apply to a standard buy-to-let purchase. If you can buy cash, then most of these go out of the window.

Simplistically, in a normal BTL purchase, you will most likely pay a minimum 25% deposit and you can rent the property out to a tenant or tenants on a standard Assured Shorthold Tenancy (AST) agreement for a period of 6-12 months, renewable after the term.

With SA, you can't necessarily use the same mortgage as a BTL. This is partly because SA is still a relatively new concept and most mortgage companies have not yet caught up with the market. This means that mortgages for SA are not as common at the moment, however, lenders are catching up fast. Because of this, normal BTL products will only give permission for the landlord to rent out the property to individuals on a normal AST agreement for a minimum of 6 months at a time. This obviously becomes a problem for people who would like to use that property for SA. I have heard stories where the local council have discovered that a landlord is renting out their property as an SA without the proper permissions in place and they then took it upon themselves to inform the landlords lender, who then promptly asked for the remainder of the mortgage to be paid in full within the next 7 days for violating the terms of the mortgage. I hope this highlights the importance of getting the right permissions in place at the time of purchase.

Using a property for SA rather than as a standard BTL is considered riskier by lenders and so, you are likely to pay a higher deposit and higher interest on a product specific to this use than on a standard BTL or residential mortgage. I have seen some lenders asking for a minimum deposit of 30% and an interest rate of around 6-8% to operate the unit as an SA. I have also heard stories of people asking for permission from their lender after purchasing as a BTL to use the property as an SA and then permission being granted. However, I believe this to be the exception rather than the rule.

Another point you will need to consider is if you are buying a freehold or a leasehold. If you are buying an apartment you will more than likely be buying a leasehold and you will also have to pay ground rent and service charges for the maintenance of the building. Because of these extra parties, you will have to seek the permission of the freeholder and management company.

Management companies are increasingly becoming aware of this strategy and are not very fond of their building being used as multiple small hotels. This is usually because of the increased maintenance that comes with high turnover of people and increased risk of parties, noise and generally causing trouble for long term tenants in the building.

If they explicitly state that their apartments are not for short-term lets and an owner goes ahead and does it anyways, they can demand for the apartment to be removed from any OTAs, returned to its intended use with all future bookings being cancelled.

Not getting the correct permissions could lead to anything from paying penalty fees, to your mortgage lender demanding a repayment of your full mortgage balance or even your freeholder forfeiting your lease and reclaiming the property.

RENTING

Renting the property to then use as SA is otherwise known as rent-to-rent or more appropriately, rent-to-SA. There are a few ways to arrange this, some examples including: a company let, management agreement or common law agreement. Due to the small amount of capital we had to start our SA venture, this is the strategy that we implemented as it doesn't require that much up front cost compared to the others.

There are two ways of finding rental properties for operating SA: either through a letting agent or direct to landlord. In my experience, letting agents aren't too familiar with company lets and need a little education from you on this. One agent, who I contacted about an apartment which I actually ended up renting, assertively told me that they did not do company lets. Once I suggested she checked, implying it's usually down to the landlord's preferences rather than the agent's, found that the landlord was fine with it so we were able to proceed.

Therefore, it's safe to say that it's much simpler to secure properties direct from the landlord than through an agent. Thankfully, landlords are increasingly becoming more attracted to the low fees and ease of letting their property through online-only letting agents such as OpenRent, Visum or PurpleBricks. These sites, alongside others such as

Gumtree, allow them to advertise their property cheaply and enable direct contact with between the interested party and the landlord so they're the ones you should be looking for.

Now that we have the ways in which to find the property you want, one thing we should clarify straight away is the type of agreement you need to use. If you are going through a letting agent, you will most likely use a company let agreement with the sub-letting clause removed. I can't emphasise enough how important it is to agree the removal of the sub-letting clause! Should you not do this, operating a SA unit from the property will violate your agreement and if the landlord, management company or letting agent find out, you may be asked to vacate the property at the first opportunity.

For those thinking they may be able to get away with renting any unit and keeping this activity hidden from any of these interested parties, remember that all it will take is for one unhappy neighbour to complain to your landlord or management company and that will be that. I heard one story where someone was operating an SA in an apartment complex and the building had a very nice concierge. On the face of it, this could be very attractive for someone looking to operate SA. However, one guest who was booked for the weekend and due to check-in at 3.00pm arrived around 1.00pm, and asked the concierge if they could check-in early. Confused, the man asked which apartment they were due to stay at and if they knew the owner to which the guests very kindly answered that they had booked the apartment through

Booking.com and they did not know the owner. The concierge informed the management company who passed the message onto the landlord and then subsequently ejected the SA operator. This hopefully shows just how easy it is for this strategy to fail if not done properly.

The basics of our agreements offer two simple (yet very attractive) things: full guaranteed rent every month and all maintenance under a certain monthly amount taken care of. I have to admit, that with the 1st property we manged to get, we were so eager to get started that we just agreed to take care of all maintenance with the apartment, regardless of the amount.

This ended up being more expensive than you might think, spending on average around £80 per month. There were months where we didn't pay for any maintenance at all, but then some where everything seemed to go wrong. One in particular comes to mind, where the immersion heater element failed (leaving guests with no hot water), several lights broke, the oven element failed (leaving guests with no working oven), the toilet broke and the bathroom door lock broke with the guest's 5-year-old inside. All of this came to over £300 and some very sympathetic but unhappy guests.

If you are struggling to get through to any landlords directly then you will have to go through a letting agent. From the outset, you will need to be upfront with the letting agents and let them know what you are doing. I have personally found this much easier to explain in person than over the phone.

What wouldn't be advised is to walk in to a letting agent and tell them that you operate holiday lets and need to sub-let a property for rent. If at some point in the conversation they challenge you on the sub-letting (which they are briefed is a very big no-no and to stay away from anyone looking to do such a thing) then it's important to highlight that sub-letting is only in violation of a standard AST agreement. Hence you would not be using an AST but a company let or common law agreement. If you are just starting out in this business with no history and you are using your brand new company, you will more than likely fail the referencing that letting agents perform as standard when letting out a property. Therefore, the letting agents will most likely ask for rent in advance to give the landlord some form of security that you will indeed pay rent. For us, they asked for a full 6 months' rent (which was our company let term) in advance, moving to monthly rent payments thereafter. This became somewhat of a blessing in disguise in our case as it allowed us to generate income unaffected by monthly rent payments and build up a healthy pot of cash.

One final thing you need to do, is ensure you get is some SA specific contents insurance (this would be for both buying or renting a property) as normal contents insurance will not pay out if they find out after the fact that you have given multiple sets of strangers a set of keys to your property and let them use it for days at a time.

SOURCING AGENTS

One thing I would like to address immediately is something which I have heard so many horror stories about and something myself in particular have had my fingers burnt on. You might actually find that I'm a bit more passionate about this section than I am about others...

There are many property investment courses ongoing at the moment and if you search or join any particular property Facebook groups or in any way suggest to Facebook that you own or are interested in property investment, then you will inevitably see an advertisement for a property investment course of some kind. These courses are obviously aimed at people who have a decent amount of capital to begin with who can afford to buy a property or two. However, there are also people who attend those courses who don't have means of investing themselves. So one thing these educators encourage those people to do is to become what is known as 'sourcing agents'. These people are generally the most novice because they have not bought any properties themselves but their role generally, is to make offers on properties and once they have an offer accepted to then sell that deal onto another investor after it's been agreed. The fees vary greatly but on average, you can expect to pay around £2,000 per property. Sometimes, the ones who can come across quite legitimate and professional will ask for a £500 deposit while they search for a property on your behalf.

What I would like to address is that there are a lot of unscrupulous or incompetent people who become sourcing agents with the aim of building enough cash to invest themselves by selling deals to other people. The property industry can become quite frustrating at times and once you become aware of these people, it may be very tempting to use their services as they can basically offer you a property on a plate. I would like to take this opportunity to tell you not to take it. I am sure there are a few competent and professional sourcing agents out there, however, I have encountered (and used) a few sourcing agents now and I can tell you from my experience, those agents are so few and far between, that it's not worth risking your money and time on them.

Sourcers have all the reasons to tell you how good a deal is and no incentive to disclose the risks involved and how it could fail. Others within the community of property investors will say that it's down to the investor to perform all the necessary due diligence and any money lost on an investment is their own fault, almost implying that if they are stupid enough to buy a bad deal from a sourcing agent, then they deserve to lose their cash. My personal advice is to steer clear.

From my point of view, if I have to perform all the due diligence on deals anyway, what am I paying the £2,000 for? Of course, there's also the fact that you won't find out all of the details of the deal until you pay a deposit which might be non-refundable if you refuse it. I would personally much rather do it myself and save my £2,000. It's easy enough to secure properties without them.

THE DEAL

Once you have found a property you think would work, that is, it's in a good location according to other guest reviews from nearby properties, and has a good enough kerb appeal it's time to assess whether or not it would be a good deal and indeed worth investing in.

As a rule of thumb, deals that meet our standard are ones that break even at 50% occupancy. So this is 15 out of 30 days occupied with at least 8 cleans from a cleaning company and around £100 cost of linen hire/week. You will obviously need to add up all of your monthly costs (mortgage or rent, electricity, water, gas, internet) and by the way, we have found that utility bills have been around 30% higher than what you would expect for normal bills (sometimes, up to 100% more when during winter months) so do allow for this. You then need to assume the highest amount of cleans per month (for us, that is calculated at an average of 2-night stays to estimate the highest costs). For example, for a property on a rent-to-rent at £800 per month, at 50% occupancy we would have the following cost:

Item	Cost/month
Rent	£800
Cleaning	£240 (£30 per changeover)
Linen	£200
Utilities	£200
Total cost	**£1,440**

If you want to break even at 50% occupancy, say 15 nights booked, then your average price per night should be £96.00. From researching our area, we found the average price per night to be £120 so the total revenue at 50% occupancy is £1800. In other words, by achieving the area's average nightly price of £120 we would make around £360 profit even if the apartment would be booked half the time. This is a pretty good deal as it could work even if we had to reduce the price to, say, £100 per night.

Obviously, it's completely up to you to set your break-even threshold as low as you feel comfortable, but it's important to set a standard and see if your deals stack up. One word of advice I would give you is not to try and force a deal. Operate on the numbers you find, not ones that you would like to achieve. Doing that will only lead to bad results. Be confident in your research because if you find a good deal, other investors will find it as well. So when you find a good deal, go for it.

THE FURNISHINGS AND AMENITIES

Once you have secured the property you need to get it furnished, and furnished to a high standard. Some people use second hand furniture and if it's in very good condition you may just be able to get away with it, but I wouldn't recommend it. Guests' standards of apartments are generally getting higher due to the increasing number of units becoming available and as I say, you may be able to get away with it, but you will risk getting poorer reviews. In the early stages of the unit being listed on the OTAs it is crucially important that your review score remains high so I wouldn't do anything that would potentially compromise this. I would therefore, recommend that you go for brand new furniture.

There are companies out there that specialise in SA furniture who provide packages specific to your property. They will also come out and furnish the entire property in one day, and the quicker it's fully furnished, the quicker you can start bringing in guests and therefore, bringing in some money.

Alternatively, you can go and buy all the furniture yourself. This is something that we have opted for especially when starting out as we wanted to be in control of the guest experience.

In terms of the style of furnishings, this is completely your decision and you should also have a good look at your competition and the general style of the other operators in the area. But if I had to define the style that we've used and that our guests have enjoyed, I would say it's a mixture between a hotel room and an Ikea scene. The hotel style bedding with the Ikea style living room, as well as all the modern amenities that people of today would be surprised if they weren't present during their stay. I would also suggest you add one thing that is a pleasant surprise for your guests (known in the customer service industry as a 'delighter'). In the past, we have used a corkboard world map placed on the wall in one of the bedrooms with pins on. This doesn't sound like much, but we put the first pin around the North West of England which is where the apartment was based, and the guests started placing pins to countries where they have come from. Another thing we have added was a box full of goodies for families and children such as colouring books with pens and crayons and board games. It's a tiny addition, but one that people definitely notice and something people remember.

With the colour scheme of the property, what we have used is mainly bland and neutral colours for the walls and furnishings (white or grey walls carpets and beds) with the small very colourful additions for impact as shown in *Image 3*. This same colour theme would apply to bedrooms, mainly neutral colours with a few solid colour contrasting bright pieces. This would also apply to pictures that you put up on the wall, the 3 small pictures above the headboard of a bed is very modern and always looks nice and is definitely a style we go for.

Image 3

If you are buying your property to use as an SA, there is a general recommendation that you get fitted furniture as it lasts much longer and generally looks much better. In this case however, you will have to think long term as you will hopefully be keeping the SA going for at least 5 years. To ensure the style doesn't look silly or dated in one or two years, it could be worth consulting a designer. In my opinion, the leading man in this area is a guy named Julian Maurice. All of his products look amazing and I would recommend you check him out, even if just for some inspiration.

As I mentioned earlier in the book, I would recommend you go for a sofa bed for the living room as this opens up your apartment to an extra two guests (you can, of course, charge for the extra inconvenience and cost of extra linen) but keep the overall colour scheme of the furniture itself neutral. No bright red leather sofas. In the downloadable 'Resources' section, you can find a complete list of everything that we used to furnish our first SA with and an estimated price total.

In terms of the amenities you need to offer, the idea is that anyone can walk into the property and not have to buy anything to make their stay comfortable. Toilet roll would be the prime example. No one would expect to have to provide their own toilet roll when they stay in an apartment. The same expectation would be there for plates, glasses, utensils, cutlery, pots and pans, kettles, microwaves, kitchen roll as well as towels, hangers, an ironing board and an iron. We offer all of these as well as complimentary tea, coffee, sugar, shower gel, shampoo, conditioner and hand soap. These and all of your other consumable items are easily found from your local Costco (if you haven't got a membership, I would highly recommend it - it's well worth the £30 per year). There are also wholesalers who will provide you with the hotel style mini bottles of shampoo, conditioner and shower gel. For us, it was more economical to have labelled dispensers for these and buy the refills in bulk from Costco. The same applies for tea, coffee, sugar and sweeteners. Individually wrapped packets are again available if that is your preference but we found it more economical to supply a full jar of each and let the guest have as much as they like during their stay.

I would strongly suggest that once you have your property at the point where you feel it's ready to bring guests in, that you stay at least one night in the property yourself. This is one of the most useful tips I have heard and it's one thing that a lot of SA operators don't actually do. Staying in the apartment yourself gives you the best insight of the guests' experience. For example, if there is a problem with the hot water system when you have a shower, you will not know until you actually take a shower. This is something you would not have otherwise known about until an unhappy guest tells you about it.

THE LINEN

One of two major items that you will need to consider when setting up your SA unit is the linen and by that I mean bathroom towels as well as bedroom linen. Some questions that may spring to mind could be:

- Where do you get it from?
- Who will clean the used bedding?
- How good quality does the bedding need to be?
- How many items will you actually need?

There are multiple ways in which people deal with these issues. Some buy their own linen and then wash it themselves after each changeover. Most often, these are small operators with possibly a bedroom in their own house or annexe that they use for SA, or those who live nearby and for whom it is more cost effective to clean their units themselves.

Others buy their own linen and then employ a cleaner to handle the changeover by taking the linen to a dry cleaner or taking the linen home with them to clean and iron, which is a service that some cleaners offer (and obviously charge extra for). There are a few problems I have with this system, the main one being that the type of bed linen you find in a normal bedding store isn't meant for heavy use or several washes per week. Therefore, it can become damaged quicker than you might think.

Another issue with this is the heavy reliance on the cleaner. I have heard stories where someone's cleaner just decided to quit and keep all the linen. The operator had a guest checking out and another checking in the same day, so they had to go out and buy all fresh linen and go to the property themselves and handle the changeover. You can only imagine the amount of stress and rush to go and get everything ready for the next guest. And what if you can't get there in time?

One final point about buying all of your own linen is that if your first guest ruins that bed sheet or bath towel then you need to go out and buy another, and if this keeps happening then you will need to keep going out and buying new linen. This is something we have avoided simply because of the number of stories I have heard where guests have used brand new plush bath towel as make up remover! (even when the host has provided a dark towel - with the words 'Make Up Remover' specifically sewn in they have still used the plush white one!). Let me tell you, waterproof mascara is forever!

The system which we have used is one where we rent hotel grade linen from a linen company which collects used and delivers new fresh, clean and pressed linen once a week to the property in lockable wheelie bins (which they provide). We have a cleaner who goes in and completes the changeover, taking the new linen into the property and placing it in storage. This seemed to us the easiest for everyone involved. It doesn't place too much reliance on one person or company and the only issues we have had so far were that every once in a while, the linen comes in stained (which we flag up and subsequently aren't charged for) or the cleaners couldn't make it because of sick leave (so we have had to complete the changeovers ourselves). But I would say that this is part and parcel of the SA world; you need a back-up plan for everything and sometimes you'll need to do it yourself. Renting the linen might cost more in the long run than buying your own, but we would not have the capacity (or the energy) to wash and iron our own linen and then deliver back to the property. The cost of hiring linen will vary greatly on how much you actually use, which of course depends on your occupancy rate and average nights per stay. We have a minimum 2 nights' stay and when we have had occupancy rate of >90%, our linen costs have been between £200-300 per month per apartment.

The last option I'm aware of which is probably the most efficient is one I think most suited to big SA operators. They can rent the linen and have it delivered to a central location, for example, the delivery area of an apartment block in a maintenance room for cleaners only. There, they sort out all the linen and take cages or trolleys of linen to the rooms for the changeovers in a very similar way to what you'd see in a hotel. There is one big operator I know of who gets all their linen delivered to a van parked in the building car park and their cleaners sort the fresh linen out in the back of one van and the used linen is collected in another van parked in the space next to it. A very clever and efficient system to use, but obviously you need multiple SA units within the same area and have some central location that can be used as a hub for sorting out all the linen for your cleaners.

How much linen you'll need at any one point depends entirely on how many changeovers you'll need to do on a given week and how often you can get the linen cleaned and fresh for the next guest. If you open up your calendar to one night bookings, then you need to be prepared to arrange seven changeovers per week. This can get either very labour intensive and/or very expensive.

We have a minimum stay of 2 nights so for any given week, we will most likely need three complete changeovers per week. The most cost effective type of guests will be professionals and contractors who stay for weeks at a time. This is because they need minimal changeovers as they are happy to keep the same linen for at least one week at a time. For guests staying for longer periods, the standard is to perform one clean and one changeover every 5-7 days during their stay.

I hope these have detailed out enough information for you to be able to make a good decision on how to solve one of the two biggest issues with SA, the linen.

THE CLEANING

As we have dealt with the first major issue when it comes to running an SA unit, now seems like an appropriate time to deal with the second: the cleaning.

Some people elect to do this themselves as they have ultimate control over their guests' experiences, they know they can do a good job and also know when a guest perhaps tells a fib to try and get a refund or some money off (it's known for some guests to make a bit of a mess and then claim the place hasn't been cleaned to get some money back, much like in hotels). Choosing to do your own cleaning will of course keep your costs down but obviously, you will sacrifice your time and you will be restricted in the number of units you can actually clean yourself. In this situation some people can become a real slave to their SA unit, not taking holidays or breaks because they either can't get or don't want to pay for cleaners. Whilst this isn't an option I would choose from the outset, it is one that I would resort to if there were no other solutions.

We use cleaning companies as they generally provide a good reliable source of cleaners and they are generally big enough to replace people if, for whatever reason, the cleaner allocated to your unit can't turn up. Cleaning companies generally provide a minimum standard and are professional in the way they do their job. While companies that offer services specifically designed for SA can be hard to find (they're generally used to cleaning offices), there are some that do understand SA and are generally very good and quite flexible with the additional duties they might have to undertake, such as filling up consumables or cleaning dishes (they will of course charge for the extra time this takes). I would say that one downfall with using a cleaning company is that when you get different cleaners, the standard may not be consistent. Therefore, by using a cleaning company you may lose an element of control of the guest experience.

Just to give you an idea of the cost of using a cleaning company, the average rate is around £13 per hour before VAT (if they incur it) and an apartment will usually take between one and two hours to clean properly, so that's around £30 per changeover.

Others choose to employ a cleaner on a zero-hour contract or ask them to declare self-employment and issue periodic invoices and pay them an hourly rate. One thing to remember immediately is that if you employ someone in your company, they are automatically entitled to all of the statutory employee benefits so you may have to deal with quite a bit of additional paperwork. The vast majority of the bigger SA operators employ their own cleaners as this becomes more cost efficient as you get additional units and based in the nearby vicinity. The average hourly rate for a cleaner is around £10 per hour and for us, the minimum number of units to have before it became economically worthwhile to employ a cleaner instead of using cleaning companies was 4. This is obviously dependant on your individual circumstances, but one thing you will gain from using employees or individual cleaners is that you will have more control over the guest experience as you will have an individual who is accountable for the standard of the property that the guests arrive at.

Whichever strategy you decide to use, make sure that you are clear about what your minimum standard is, exactly what you'd like the cleaner to do, and specifically, how you'd like the property to be arranged. Perhaps organise a checklist or cleaning manual with pictures to help.

One thing we have also done is give the cleaners an extra set of keys. Whilst this has never happened to us, we have heard multiple stories where a guest has taken the keys with them and the host, being the only other key holder, was out of the country or hours away. This meant that the apartment could not be cleaned and that the next guest could not gain access to the property.

In terms of running an SA unit day-to-day, these two issues, the linen and the cleaning will amount to the vast majority of issues that you'll need to be sorting out.

THE MARKETING

Now that you have decided on a property, have secured it for SA use and fully furnished it, it's time to think about how best to market your unit. The marketing of your SA unit is absolutely crucial. How you market your unit will ultimately determine firstly the success of your unit, and secondly, the type of guests you will get staying in the property.

For example, if you advertise your unit entitled 'Good Time Central' allowing up to 8 people, are based in a big city centre, allow one night stays and have pictures showing a big living room with a pool table and minibar, you will most likely get people looking to have a good party. If this is your target market then by all means go with this, Lord knows that there are plenty of SA units out there on the OTAs that do not allow partying so if there was a way to allow people to party then that could be a lucrative strategy. The down side to this is the vastly increased expected maintenance and cleaning bills.

However, if you advertise the same unit as 'Lovely Family Home' allowing up to 4 guests and then charge an extra £30 per extra person per night, have a minimum 2 or 3 night stay with pictures showing a very nice comfortable bed, some colouring books and a high chair, then you will most likely have families staying in your unit. You may still get someone booking for a party, but not many parties last for longer than one night and paying the extra £30 to house the extra people can become very expensive for a party.

I hope these two examples help show the difference in the marketing will drive the type of guests you will attract and to help keep the cleaning and maintenance costs down.

PHOTOS

If the marketing is absolutely crucial to the success of your SA unit, then the photos are just as crucial to successful marketing. For all of those cheap landlords who don't quite see the value in photographers I will explain this very simply. You need a professional photographer to take pictures of your unit. Either that or you need to buy a high quality camera and do this yourself, but a photo shoot will definitely be cheaper and they can do wonders with editing the photos afterwards which most people won't know how to do.

Depending on where you go, professional photo shoots can be £100-£300 but they are definitely worth the money. In terms of the photos to include in your listing, you need photos of absolutely everything and then of the outside and nearby towns and attractions. Most OTAs allow you to put as many photos as you'd like on their website and they all have a minimum. Once uploaded they also perform a check on the quality of the photos uploaded and will reject some which aren't good enough quality, so sorry, no you can't get away with pictures from your mobile phone or iPad.

For comparison, *Image 4* was taken with my iPhone and *Image 5* was taken by a professional photographer. I'm not sure exactly what the photographer did differently apart from the angle, but the latter image is definitely brighter and more inviting than the first photo (and yes, I did get rid of that couch before guests arrived).

Image 4

Image 5

It's amazing really how small subtle differences can make such a difference and create such different impressions on the same place.

As a rule of thumb, get as many high quality photos of your unit taken and add photos of nearby attractions. I would also trust your gut instinct when deciding which photos to upload from the selection that the photographer gives you (as there will most likely be around 50). There may be something you just don't like about a picture that you cannot articulate but just doesn't look right. If you don't think it looks right, neither will a potential guest.

As another small tip, after you have had a few guests who have left you some great reviews, add some quotes to your photos description. For example, we have a picture of one of our plush beds and in the description (which appears on the photo) is a quote from one of our guests saying - 'Beds are sooo comfy!' - Megan, July 2018. This is great for adding that little extra touch to let people know about the things that people loved about your property when they stayed there without going through the reviews, or reviews on other platforms.

DESCRIPTIONS

The descriptions are probably the third most important part of your advertising (if I were to rank them in order). This is your chance to really grab your target market and reassure them that your place is where they want to stay.

There are restrictions on the descriptions that you can give. For example, at the time of writing, AirBnB have a 500-character limit on your description but then encourage you to add more detail in other sections such as 'The Space' which doesn't have a limit. So you can go into as much detail as you'd like about the furnishings and other services you provide.

Booking.com will provide the descriptions for you after you fill out a fairly long tick box style form. This is something you will need to double-check though as they will sometimes get things wrong. We once listed a property in Chester and on the actual listing it appeared in Chesterfield, so if you searched in Chesterfield you would have found our apartment and when selected, it would have the property address in Chester! Imagine that. So we had to contact them directly to resolve this issue which actually took around 2 weeks to resolve.

THE CHECK-IN PROCESS

If I could make one recommendation for the check-in process summed up in four words, those words would be 'the simpler, the better!'.

There are a wealth of options available to hosts on exactly how to check-in their guests and there are temptations to complicate the process in the attempt to simplify and systemise it. We will go through the many options available so you can make an educated decision on this but my personal view is that the process needs to be simple, flexible, sustainable and most importantly, convenient for the guests.

We keep the check-in process very simple. I see many, many operators who provide their check-in details in an email to the guest at around 2,000 words long. These are the same operators who then complain that guests don't follow instructions and don't read the emails they've been sent. I have to be honest, I wouldn't be bothered to read a 2,000-word essay on how to get to the property, then how to access the keys etc. and would you? Something to bear in mind is that hotels just provide you the address to their hotel and that's about it. What does the guest have to do? Turn up. The simplest thing they can do (and sometimes guests get delayed and have issues with that!) and as I've said previously, they aren't quite directly your competition, but you are competing indirectly with them.

I think the first question you have to ask yourself is do you want to operate a self-check-in, or meet 'n greet process? As always, there are positives and negatives to both.

SELF-CHECK-IN

The typical self-check-in process is where the guest arrives in the area and gains access to the property without meeting the host, put simply, by doing everything themselves. The big bonus with this is flexibility, for both guests and host.

Guests can check-in whenever they arrive (as long as it's during the check-in period), which is very attractive as they can have flexibility with their travel arrangements. A potential downside is that this can also apply for checking out. If you have a check-out time of 9am I wouldn't be surprised if guests actually left later than this. Another bonus for this is guests can feel more at home and welcome as they have the place to themselves although on the flip side, some may get confused over how things work in the property.

One potential negative aspect to self-check-in is security and the fact that you can never be 100% sure the guest who booked is the one who is staying; unless you put a system in place to make it very unlikely that it is anybody else. Some of the systems that are available for people looking to operate a self-check-in process are detailed in the downloadable 'Resources'.

MEET 'N GREET

The typical meet 'n greet process is where the guest is greeted at the property by someone who is very familiar with the property (this is usually the host) who checks them in, shows them around the place and answers any potential questions they may have. They also typically meet them at around the check-out time to collect the keys and check the property when the guests leave.

The major benefit with this is security. You can be 100% sure that the person who booked is also the person who is staying, that the number of guests in the booking is actually the number of guests staying. As there is someone present at the time of arrival and at the time of check-out, you can also be certain that any damage found was caused by the guest checking out and therefore, claim through the OTA or deduct from the deposit accordingly.

The main negative to this is the cost of having someone present at check-in and/or check-out. There are, of course, companies who will provide people to perform this service for around £30 or you may choose to check the guests in yourself. If you do choose the latter option, however, you will have to decide at some point whether you want to grow the business and in doing so, get others to do it for you.

Another downside is that meet n' greet restricts the flexibility of the guests in relation to their arrival time (unless you or others would be happy to greet guests at 11.30pm). Therefore, you need to arrange when the guests can arrive and then hope they turn up on time. I have known operators who have been left waiting around for a few hours for guests to arrive as their travel arrangements changed.

OUR CHECK-IN PROCESS

We have properties in apartment buildings that have electronic gated access to the building, then a key box in the doorway of the apartment itself. Once inside, they check-in with a 'Welcome' tablet which also has full explanations of how things work inside the apartment.

We have chosen self-check-in so that our guests can check-in any time after 3pm. On the morning of the check-in, we text the guest directly to their mobile phone the full address, then the code to the building with a video of the code being punched into the entry system, then the code for the key box with a video showing the code being punched in and accessing the keys. With hundreds of guests, we have only had one call requesting further clarification and even then, the guest wanted directions to find the building and didn't struggle with the check-in itself. This works for us but may not be appropriate for you and as always, it will depend on your circumstances and the type of property.

THE ADMIN STUFF

Before you can list your property online, there's a few admin things that you need to put in place. Whilst this might not be everyone's reason to get out of bed in the morning, it's definitely as important as all the practical (and more fun) stuff.

HEALTH AND SAFETY

Similar to a buy-to-let landlord, you have a duty of care towards your guests and as such, are required to make reasonable efforts to ensure they are safe within the property during their stay.

Starting from the obvious, this would be a lockable front door to their property, or if they are in a room of a house, a lockable door. Ensuring that all appliances have been PAT tested by a certified engineer and that gas safety checks have been carried out is also good practice. Whilst you are not obligated to present these to the guests when they check-in, if something goes wrong you may have to provide these as evidence of exercising due care. Other fairly obvious things will be having things such as smoke detectors throughout, a fire blanket in the kitchen and if you have a gas boiler, a carbon monoxide detector. All of these of course need to be at the required standard and in good working order.

Moving onto the not so obvious things you will need, if you have an immersion heater or any water tank, you will need to have a legionella risk assessment performed. Don't worry, you don't need to have a certified risk assessor, this can be done yourself, but you will need to actually do it and record the outcome and any improvements you have noticed while performing the risk assessment. This also applies for a general risk assessment of the property. It's considered good practice to have these performed yearly and I would suggest you do at least one yourself as it gets you into the safety conscious mind set. If you have never performed one in your life, then maybe get the first one done by a certified risk assessor and be present while they carry it out so you get an understanding of their thinking. You will have to have a separate fire risk assessment performed and recorded and if it's a house you may need to think about fire escapes if renting individual rooms. We have also invested in some glow in the dark, self-adhesive fire exit signs and put them up above the exit door, then again on the walls anywhere where you can't see the exit door so that if the electricity went and there is a fire, the guests can still evacuate safely.

Apart from these sorts of risk assessments, you will need to outline an escape plan for your guests in case of fire. This will look something similar to the one provided in *Image 6*.

Property name - Emergency Plan

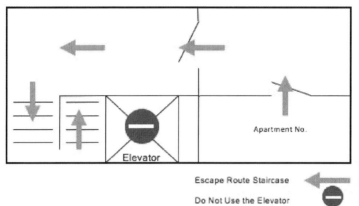

Apartment No.

Escape Route Staircase

Do Not Use the Elevator

On Discovery of a Fire in the Apartment

- Stay Calm
- Alert other people in the apartment
Call 999
- Close windows and doors to prevent fire spreading
- Do not stop to collect personal items
- Close the front door on exit
- Try to warn adjacent or adjoining flats and residents
- Do not use the elevator
- Calmly exit the building via the main stairs
- Contact property manager on XXXXXXXXXXX
- Do not go back into building until Fire and Rescue Services informs you it is safe to do so
- Muster point is located in the Car Park

Image 6

It would also be considered good practice if you provided a first aid kit as well as a sign on the door to where it's stored. On a number of occasions, guests have contacted me with an incident, usually with their children, who were in need of a first aid kit or the hospital.

This brings me to another information sheet which I would recommend: a local information sheet with the phone numbers and locations of local emergency services as shown in *image 7*.

Your Apartment Address
Apartment No.
Building Name
Street
City
Post Code

Contact Numbers for Insight Serviced Apartment Staff
Company name mobile - emergency only   XXXXXXXXXXX

Your local Accident and Emergency Services

Fire Brigade   Emergency   999

Cheshire Police   Emergency   999
Chester Town Hall Police Station   Enquiries   101
Northgate Street
Chester
CH1 2HJ

Countess of Chester Hospital   Emergency   999
Liverpool Road   Non-emergency   111
Chester   Hospital Reception   01244 366663
CH2 1UL   Accident and Emergency 01244 365000

Emergency Dentist
Deva Dental Clinic   24 Hour Emergency   01244 377373
4 Liverpool Road
Chester
CH2 1AE

Further information on local services are provided on your Welcome tablet

Image 7

It wouldn't do any harm if you provided signs such as 'Caution. Please take care due to slippery floor' or 'Caution. Water can get very hot' near the hot water taps. It's quite easy to go over the top with these things but if you have ever been sued for compensation because a guest has suffered a burn from using the hot water taps then people learn to go over the top to avoid liability rather than encourage people to use common sense. Thankfully (touch wood) we haven't yet been sued for such a thing but the possibility is always there. These information sheets need to be displayed clearly and in a place that the guests won't miss them. We always have them framed and then hang them up on the wall of the corridor as soon as you enter the property with the escape plan on the back of the front door, all at eye level.

YOUR POLICIES

It's imperative that you get your policies in order before you begin taking any bookings as they are your recourse if (heaven forbid) anything goes wrong with a guest.

It's like the statutory rights you have when you buy something in a shop or rent a car. If someone wants a refund or crashes their rental car, these policies detail what happens, who is liable for what and very specifically, how much will be charged for penalties, deposit, and what happens if either party cancels; things of that nature.

I want to go through the standard T&Cs so you get an understanding of what needs to be detailed in them. There are quite a few sections which are fairly self-explanatory but still need to be explained in your T&Cs. You can find our full T&Cs in the 'Resources' download. Just as a note, you should get your own T&Cs written up by your own property solicitor. The details of the T&Cs below are just my interpretations and summations of the General T&Cs.

You would expect to see the following sections (in one form or another) in any set of T&Cs.

BOOKING AND PAYMENT PROCEDURE

Detailed in this section is exactly how you will take payment, how long before the stay payment will be taken and how their card details (if taking card payments) will be handled. It would also detail how payment will be taken for recurring and/or prolonged stays (usually 4 weeks or more). Also detailed in this section are details of the security deposit, including how much you will be taking (if any) and when it's likely to be returned.

CANCELLATION POLICY

This section explains what happens if a cancellation by either party is made and what bookings (if any) are refundable.

AMENDMENTS TO A BOOKING

This section details what happens if the guest or the host amends the booking and also details what happens if the guest leaves early or extends the booking and incurs any extra cost in doing so.

FACILITIES AND SERVICES

This section details what services you or your company are responsible for and what is included in the stay. The prime example of this type of service is complimentary internet and Wi-Fi access.

NUMBER OF OCCUPANTS

As you would expect, this section details how many people are allowed to stay in the apartment on any given night and that you hold the right to refuse entry for anyone who breaches this number.

CHECK-IN, CHECK-OUT AND RETURN OF KEYS

We use check-in from 3.00pm and check-out at 10.00am and I would say that around these times are fairly standard. Most people offer check-in between around 1.00-4.00pm and check-out from 9.00am to 12.00pm. This will obviously depend on your comfort level and also how much time between stays you feel your cleaners would need. Remember to give yourself some flexibility in case your cleaners are delayed or for whatever reason can't make it. This is also the section to detail any charges you might apply for any lost or damaged keys, fobs, parking permits or any other items you provide as part of your check-in and/or check-out procedure. Finally, this is the place to mention what might be charged for late return of keys or delays in leaving the property as well as what happens to any items left in the property after the guests have left.

DAMAGES TO APARTMENT AND PAYMENT OF ADDITIONAL CHARGES

This is possibly where the solicitor really earns their fee as it's the one that gives you financial protection against damages. Here, you might explain what might be charged and what for. Usually, this encompasses everything from general cleaning (and how much a general cleaning fee will be) to how much will be charged if the property is left in disrepair. This usually involves charging the guest for loss of revenue if another guests' stays need to be cancelled. One other thing to note is that this is both for individual guests and guests staying on behalf of a company.

LIABILITY

This section is quite simple and just details what liability you or your business has in terms of the guests' belongings during their stay, which will essentially say that things happen in life and you cannot be held liable if their stuff gets stolen or broken during their stay in the property.

LAW AND JURISDICTION

Another simple section here as it just details which country's law this contract is subject to in the event of a dispute. For us, this is England and Wales.

TERMINATION BY (YOUR COMPANY NAME)

This section simply details under which circumstances you may wish to terminate a guests stay after they have already checked in.

INJURY OR LOSS

As you'd expect, this details the fact that you are not liable for any injury or loss incurred during the stay.

RIGHTS OF ACCESS

Something which is quite unique to SA is the fact that you or any subcontractor are allowed to access the property at any point with regard to the guest. This is required as you may need immediate access to the property for any kind of maintenance issue, but also if you wish to evict the guest, something which is definitely not permitted under any other kind of property rental agreement.

PETS

As you would expect, this would detail if you allow any pets in the property during the guests' stay. Most hosts don't as it's got potential to cause real headaches but it does seem that hosts in America are more open to the idea. I'm not sure if the trend will migrate over the pond any time soon.

One word of warning regarding pets is that there are provisions within OTA agreements where they cannot refuse a booking because of a pet that is required by the guest, such as a guide dog for the blind or pets for emotional support.

There have been numerous cases where a host has been penalised for not accepting a booking from a guest because they did not want a guest staying in their property with their emotional support animal. I think the animal in question was a large dog, but AirBnB (the OTA) did not care as they regarded this as discrimination.

We include this in our T&Cs but it's worth noting that you may not be able to refuse a guest's stay based on their support animal.

SMOKING

All that is required in this section is whether or not smoking is permitted and the penalties (if any) for doing so. There are some operators I know who charge upwards of £200 for evidence of smoking and to be fair to them, the smell can be very off putting and lingers in the air for a very long time.

COMPLAINTS

In this section there is normally just a short and simple statement on the process the guest should follow if wished to make a complaint and how long after their stay they may raise such a complaint.

This is a section that's worth detailing, but there is no real ombudsman scheme or anything like that in the world of SA. The usual contract terms apply but in terms of customer recourse, the OTAs will come down hard on you if you have an unhappy guest but they don't really have the authority to' give the guest a refund on your behalf. They can of course delist your property or relegate it to the bottom of the searches though.

The vast majority of guests will not make a complaint but rather leave a very poor review if they are unsatisfied and the OTAs will generally support their review (even if the review is made up or they haven't stayed in the property). So while there is no real procedure for complaints, there are other methods of hurting your business that is well within the power of the guest.

INFORMATION

This section is just a short disclaimer to say that the information given to guests before, during or after their stay is given in good faith but you aren't liable for any inaccuracies.

INTEREST

This is the kind of interest that is accrued on a bank balance rather than interest in anything else and is applicable for late invoices or remaining balances at the end of a guest's stay.

SECURITY OF TENURE

In here is provided a short statement that any stay is exempt from the Rent Act and no tenancy is provided, therefore, you reserve the right to enter the property and vacate the guest at any point without prior notice.

USAGE AND NUISANCE BEHAVIOUR

A section is required detailing what will happen in the event of improper use (such as a party) or nuisance behaviour (such as playing loud music). This is usually in the form of penalty fines to be deducted from the deposit or the card used to make the booking.

PROPERTY SPECIFICATION

A similar statement is placed in this section detailing how the property has been advertised with reasonable care and that you aren't liable for any misrepresentation caused by the listing on other OTAs and that all information regarding the property has been supplied in good faith.

DISCOUNT/PROMOTIONAL CODES

A small paragraph is usually detailed regarding the use of discount or promotional codes (if provided).

INCLUDED AS STANDARD

A small paragraph detailing the items that may be provided (but aren't required) for the guests' stay and that if anything is removed from any storage space, the guest will be charged an amount per item. This just gives you some security in case a guest really goes rummaging through your storage spaces and cleans out your 6 months' supply of tea bags.

ACCEPTANCE OF TERMS AND CONDITIONS/CONTRACT OF HIRE

To conclude, a final statement just detailing that all terms and conditions are required to be accepted prior to arrival and payment in full of the fee and/or the deposit is regarded as acceptance of these conditions.

CONCLUSION

I know this wasn't the most exciting section and it may seem like a lot of words detailing a lot of obvious stuff, but you need to have these things detailed out because if you don't, you won't be able to claim anything if required. It's also worth knowing the kind of things that should be in your terms and conditions so that if you do get a solicitor to write up a contract for you, you will have at least some idea what should be included.

GETTING YOUR PROPERTY ONLINE

In this section we will briefly go through the three main OTAs that are associated with SA bookings and then we will go through my personal recommendation for creating your own website and bringing in bookings without paying any commission. The three main sites that we will go through are AirBnB, Booking.com and Expedia as all three work very differently from each other and you will need a good understanding of not only the process of listing your property but the payment process as well. We will go through the payments system later but for now let's focus on getting your property listed online.

Full guides to getting your property listed on these sites are provided in the Resources download.

AIRBNB

In my opinion, AirBnB is the most user friendly as it was initially designed for normal people to list their properties on the website for guests to use, whereas the others were initially set up for Hotels only and have since expanded into the SA market due to the increasing demand for SA units.

You will need to create your listing by firstly specifying your type of property then inputting a description (remembering to think about the type of guest you'd like in your property!) and then put its exact location. Once you have done this, you will need to upload some professional photos of the interior and the building itself, providing a recommended minimum of 8 photos to which you can add captions to further enhance your listing's potential.

Once this is all setup, you will be asked to set up a host profile. This is more important than you might initially think because of the culture that AirBnB promotes, encouraging people to get to know each other a little in a similar way to Facebook. Guests who are split between which property to stay, are more likely to book with hosts who have a full profile set up and seem welcoming and who also appear to enjoy hosting.

BOOKING.COM

Booking.com is actually a much quicker process than AirBnB to get your property listed online and they do most of the legwork for you. All you have to do is sign up, get your location and images sorted and they do the rest as they do your description for you.

Most of the set-up though with Booking.com is done after your property is listed with them. When listed, if you go to the 'Property' tab of the extranet there are a whole host of options for you to add to your listing, all of which you fill out as a long tick box exercise. Things from pool tables, lift access and minibar to saunas, swimming pools and a concierge.

This will definitely take an afternoon or so of your time to get everything included and set up properly but once it's all filled in you can leave it and Booking.com will give you a

Property Page score out of 100 and also give you tips on how to make things better. There is also a profile of you as the operator and Booking.com do ask you to fill it out but I have to say that we haven't and it doesn't seem to affect people making bookings. It's in Booking.com's interest for you to get as many bookings as possible so they will help you as much as they can along the way.

EXPEDIA

Expedia is much simpler again to getting your property listed. It's only really a 3 or 4 step process of signing up to Expedia and putting a property name and location. After this they send you a confirmation link and then its listed. Simple as that.

Obviously though, you will need to do everything after it's listed and Expedia are nowhere near as helpful with your listing when compared to Booking.com or AirBnB. You will need to do everything yourself. If you visit your Expedia Partner Central Extranet and go onto the 'property details' tab there are similar tabs to provide information on Property and Room Amenities, Policies and Deposits and Photos. As with Booking.com Expedia will give you a content score of your property page and a comparison to your competitors.

SYNCHING YOUR CALENDARS

To ensure that you do not get two bookings for the same date for your listing and have this performed automatically so that you don't need to manually update your listing calendars on the different OTAs when a booking comes in, you need to synchronise your calendars.

Thankfully, the OTAs have worked together on this and made the process very simple. To fully connect your online calendars, say between Booking.com and AirBnB, starting from the Booking.com extranet, you need to Export your calendar from Booking.com to AirBnB. Then Import your calendar from AirBnB to Booking.com to ensure they are connected to each other. The steps are shown in *Images 8, 9 and 10* below.

Export Calendar

Copy this link and paste it in your other site's (e.g. Airbnb, HomeAway) import calendar area. If you need more assistance, check out our FAQs.

◉ Sync my bookings and days I'm closed
○ Sync my bookings

https://admin.booking.com/hotel/hoteladmin/ical.html?t=Lkdu8NqIC   Copy link

Close

Image 8

The link in *Image 8* is copied and pasted into the 'Calendar Address' in *Image 9*.

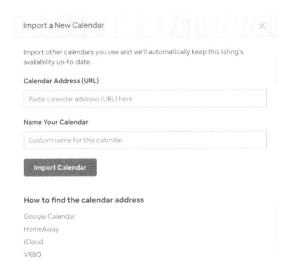

Image 9

Once this is pasted into the 'Calendar Address' box and you have given it the appropriate name, select 'Import Calendar'. After this, you will just need to Export your AirBnB calendar to Booking.com.

Image 10

When you select 'Export Calendar', you will be given a link and as before, Copy and Paste this link into the 'Calendar

URL' as shown in *Image 11* when you select to Import a calendar on the Booking.com Extranet.

Import New Calendar   ✕

If you use any other sites (e.g. Airbnb, HomeAway), copy the iCal link from that site and paste it below to keep your availability accurate. Make sure to use the calendar's iCal link – if you're not sure where to find it, check your other site's FAQs section.

Calendar URL

Paste link here

Name Your Calendar

Name your imported calendar

Close   Import calendar

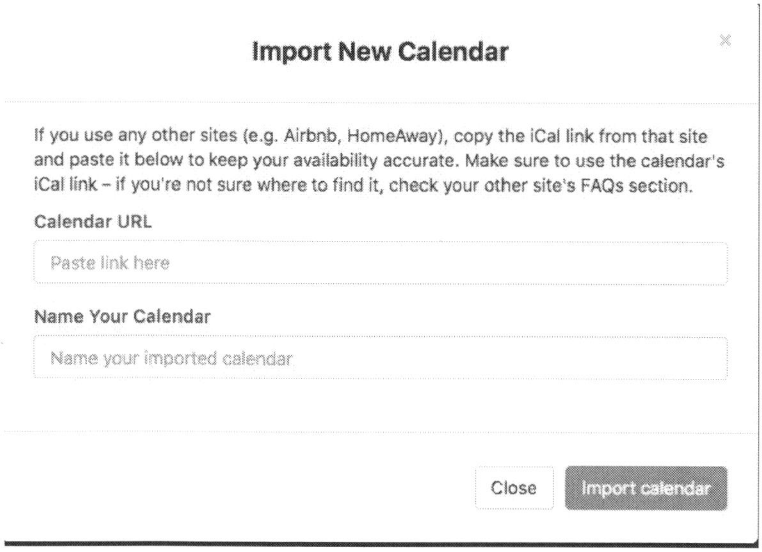

Image 11

Once you have pasted the AirBnB link into the Booking.com Extranet and Imported the Calendar, your calendars will be fully synchronised and will prevent double bookings.

OWN WEBSITE

For those of you looking to take direct bookings and keep your commission fees, then setting up your own website would be a good way to get the ball rolling. When we initially started looking into this, we consulted with three different web design companies and got some quotations for a website that had its own booking system with synch-able calendars and HD images for at least 5 listings.

The first quotation came back at around £10,500 and would take around 3 months to build. The second came back at around £7,250 and would take between 8-10 weeks and the third came back at £4,500 and would take around 12 weeks to build.

After I received all three I thought 'This is absolutely insane! How can it be so expensive?'. This is when I found Wix.com. Wix.com is a platform where you can build your own website and it has recently enabled an application called 'Wix Hotels' which has its own booking and synch-able calendar systems built in. This is free to set up and start at £3 a month at the end of your month trial. This includes your own website address so it isn't something like 'www.yourhotel.wix.com' if its available on the web, it will be 'www.yourhotel.com' making it look much more professional.

I would highly recommend going this route instead of through a web design agency. We would have to have the website for at least 29 years before it made economic sense to go with the cheapest web design agency. For us it was simply a no-brainer.

KEEP THINGS SIMPLE

If could offer a word of advice when it comes to dealing with guests, it would be just to keep things simple. This is more applicable to potential guests coming from AirBnB than any other OTA but I have also experienced this kind of thing on Expedia.

On AirBnB, they have a feature called 'Instabook', this is where if a guest wants to stay in your property on a given date, and the date is free in your calendar, then they can pay and book instantly - as long as they meet your booking requirements. Our requirements for bookings are quite simple, as the potential guest must:

- Have government ID uploaded
- Have a confirmed phone number
- Have a confirmed email address
- Provide payment information
- Agree to house rules

As long as guests tick all of these boxes, they can book instantly. There are additional requirements that you can ask for, such as:

- Recommendation from other hosts
- Guest trip information

The alternative to this is that the guest requests to book, then you can go through all of the relevant information before they book, but I find that this just discourages guests to book in the first place.

Now, on AirBnB you will get people who, for one reason or another, will not meet all of your requirements but will ask to stay in your place anyways. I won't speculate on why they wouldn't have all of these necessary information uploaded onto AirBnB, but I would always assume that there is a reason why they wouldn't want to provide such information. What they do instead is send you an enquiry for the date which they would like to stay, then provide a story and hope you accept their enquiry.

What we have always done and I would suggest you do the same, is just firstly, ask yourself why would someone ask to stay in your place (that's available to book on the calendar) when they can just do it themselves without asking? Almost every time it has been because they did not have one or multiple items on the requirements for booking instantly.

Sometimes (especially in the early days) operators can get blinded by the fact that someone wants to book that they will accept any enquiry that comes along because they are eager to get the money coming in. I would suggest that you just check why someone would enquire when they can book instantly?

Sometimes they are just simple enquiries such as - We are looking at your place and wondering what the parking is like near your apartment? But as the parking information is detailed in the listing, these are a rarity and has been much more common that people are either looking for some money off, or (the overwhelming majority of enquiries) because they don't meet the Instabook requirements.

By keeping things simple, you screen out these people automatically by just asking them to ensure their profile has all of the above then they can book instantly and do not require us to do anything for them.

SETTING YOUR PRICE

Once you have your property online you will need to decide what price you are going set for each night. You should at least have an average price per night for the area from your research so that is your starting point. Most operators will have different rates for weekdays and weekends and for SA purposes, weekdays are Sunday - Thursday and weekends are Friday and Saturday nights.

If you have furnished your property with new and/or modern furniture and expect to get at least 4/5 or 9.0/10.0 then you should be looking at higher than average prices per night for the area as you offer a premium service. Remember to keep an eye out for any events happening in your area and benchmark yourself against local competitors for how much they are charging and adjust accordingly.

One thing to be mindful of on AirBnB is a thing called Smart Pricing. This is where AirBnB set your prices for you. The concept is that you input your minimum and maximum prices per night, then according to the demand in the area, AirBnB will adjust your nightly rate accordingly. A word of warning around this: it's in AirBnB's interest to get you to set a low rate in order to secure more bookings and therefore, more commission. This approach reflects in their recommended price per night but please take this recommendation with a pinch of salt. For example, in our area, they recommended around £64 per night (for any night of the week) for a 2 bed apartment that can accommodate 6 people. We do use Smart Pricing on AirBnB but our minimum is set for around £100. AirBnB keep recommending that we reduce the price per night by £30 to secure more bookings, but the bookings are coming in anyway. The idea is always to get the maximum price for your unit per night (if this wasn't self-evident). I have seen cases where AirBnB have recommended that a host reduces their nightly rate from $24 to $9 to secure more bookings. Now that really is bargain basement stuff. $24 is already way too low but because the host owned the property outright and did everything herself so had very little running costs, she went for it. This highlights that no matter what price you set (even the recommended one!) they will always recommend that you go lower.

COMPETITION

From your research you should have a good idea who your competition is. You should have a look at their listings and also their prices and reviews. Can you undercut them and still make a tidy profit? You need to remember especially when starting out that you are brand new to the market and most people want certainty of their experience when they buy. This explains why people stay loyal to brands even when competitors offer cheaper and sometimes better quality products. As you have no reviews, you will be a question mark until that changes.

INITIAL PROMOTION

One good way to make this situation change and bring in the guests is with an initial promotion of your listing. Pretty much all of the OTAs suggest you do an initial promotional offer to your first guests as a way of enticing people to book. AirBnB do this as one of the last stages of listing your property and is around 20% off the listed price. This is, of course, optional but has worked in the past for us.

One thing to remember is that as your listing is brand new with no reviews, when users search your area for places to book, yours will almost always show towards the bottom of the list. Running an initial promotion (or any promotion afterwards) is a good way of getting your place to the top of the list. This has its own drawbacks because you are giving 20% away on top of your 8% or 15% commission fees plus all of the other bills that are incurred through running an SA unit. Your property will appear right at the top of the list, usually with a different colour box around it which makes it obvious to users that it's a paid promotion and an artificial result. Users might move past it to the 3rd or 4th result on the list which is the first 'organic' result, however, many will consider it and book your place anyways.

DEPOSIT OR NO DEPOSIT

The eternal question: to charge or not to charge a security deposit? Many operators who are already established will be thinking 'why on earth wouldn't you charge a deposit? Surely it's a no-brainer.' We don't. Some people completely disagree with this and think we are putting ourselves at risk for not doing so and they could be perfectly correct in their thinking.

I believe it's a deterrent to users looking to book with your property, especially when you're new. Some operators charge a £500 deposit. This means that for a 2-night stay for which they charge £400 they are effectively charging £900 at the time of booking. Would you have the money or be willing to pay that just for a 2-night stay? Even if you will probably get your deposit back after check-out, I would still imagine the answer is 'no'.

Secondly, most hotels don't charge a security deposit. The ones that do are usually 5 star and whose guests can most likely afford effectively paying twice the price of the stay.

Thirdly, I am not convinced that you will be able to claim anything from the deposit through the OTAs. If you are taking bookings directly, this is, of course, a different matter as it's a private contract between you and the guest. However, when an OTA is involved, they have every reason to side with the guest and you will need to provide them with evidence of the guest's wrongdoing and proof that they are responsible.

I have heard of stories where guests have left red-hot pots and pans on the solid oak kitchen counters leaving large burn marks. The quote to replace the counter came to around $400 (this is in the USA and it was a big counter). The guests denied any wrongdoing, saying the marks were there prior to their stay. The host sent all of this information to AirBnB requesting a deduction from the guest's deposit but they refused.

Even worse, the guest then left a poor review saying the host tried to scam them out of an extra $400. So the host had to fork out the $400 for the new counter top and got a poor review to show for it.

I would recommend that you charge a security deposit for direct bookings as you know 100% that you can deduct what you like from that according to your policy. Otherwise, unless you take payments directly from Booking.com (which we don't), I'm not convinced that it's actually worth doing. As with all things there are pros and cons and there are never any solutions, only trade-offs, but you need to be aware of as much as possible so you make an informed decision. It's completely up to you how you want to approach it.

I have to say though, as much 'at risk' as people may think that we are operating, the most damage that has been done by a guest after hosting hundreds, is chipping a large chunk off of the corner of a glass table and making it unsafe. Our handyman repaired the pane and the cost was around £20. I am sure guests have taken extra towels, tea bags etc. at some point but never enough to actually notice.

STAY PATIENT

There's one final thing I would like to mention about setting the price and having your initial promotions and a tip in general when running SA: stay patient!

Let's imagine that you have just put your first listing online, everything is ready or you are finishing the last few things off and are now primed, ready and waiting for someone to make that very first booking. The first day goes by without a booking. Then the second. By the third day you are becoming worried and questioning if you have done everything correctly or if your research was good enough. Maybe there's something wrong with the listing? Are the pictures okay? Yep, they're okay and your descriptions are good! But other listings are booked and yours is showing up within the first few search results. Why hasn't anyone booked yet? By the fourth day you are sitting looking at your listing and then you decide that your price is maybe too high, even with the promotion so let's drop that by another 20% shall we? STOP!

This will, more than likely, happen at some point while running your SA and you will become very tempted to start slashing prices because, after all, who can resist a bargain when they need somewhere to stay? But remember, if you are competitive with your quality and pricing, then the bookings will come. You just need to stick with it, have a little faith in the process and your listing and wait it out.

I remember with our first apartment, we waited around 5 days for our first booking which came for the following week, but then as soon as that was booked, within a few hours, another booking came in for the very next day for 3 nights. Breathe a big sigh of relief. Guests have booked and paid. Money is coming in. Again, have a little faith in the process and some confidence in your listing, the bookings will come in.

FINAL PRICING TIPS

In this section, I will offer you some final tips with your pricing which you may or may not agree with, but are practices that other operators adopt to boost their income just that little bit more.

Firstly, the cleaning fee. Always charge a cleaning fee for at least the cost of cleaning the whole property by a professional cleaner, even if you do this yourself. Guests are more than accustomed to paying a cleaning fee now for staying in someone else's property so always charge one. We charge £30 per stay but this fee varies greatly between operators and depending on the size of the property others charge up to around £40 for an apartment. Personally, I think that £40 is the upper limit of what may be adequate so your guests don't feel like they're being ripped off.

Secondly, for Booking.com, you can add other charges to your guest without paying extra commission. Under the 'Property' tab, then 'VAT/Tax/Charges' you can add any number of charges that may apply to your city. One in particular is a service charge. If you add a service charge to your listing and charge an additional 15% (equal to that of your commission) then you can essentially get the guest to pay your commission for you. Some disagree with the ethics of this practice and I can sympathise because there is no real reason for this charge and is simply a way of reducing your commission, but as guests are willing to pay it and we haven't had any complaints or even questions regarding this extra charge, we have implemented it.

Thirdly, sticking with Booking.com, if you combine this service charge with signing up to the 'Preferred Partner Program' which basically gives you better marketing and listing in the search for an extra 3% commission, you can remain high in the search results, get a nice yellow thumbs up next to your name which is a Booking.com seal of approval and pay less commission than you would normally, then it's a complete win-win. Image 12 is an image of our listing ranking since joining the 'Preferred Partner Program'.

Image 12

GETTING PAID

In this section we will go through the different systems of payment from each OTA that we have discussed. it's crucial that you are aware of any differences between their set up because problems here could lead to you not getting paid at all. We had an issue with our first Expedia guest because we were unsure of how the payment system worked and we assumed they paid us after the guest had stayed, when in fact, we had to take payment within 7 days of the booking being made. The guest had booked 2 months in advance and we waited for a £450 payment which never came. It was only when we chased Expedia that we realised that we were meant to take payment within 7 days of the booking being confirmed. We contacted the guest directly (one additional benefit of keeping guests contact details securely!) who was very understanding and paid us directly even though she didn't have to. She could quite easily have said that we should have taken payment at the time and we would have lost that money.

AIRBNB

AirBnB is probably the better system of payment out of any OTA as payment is sent 24 hours after the guest checks in. AirBnB advise that it can take up to 14 days after check-in for the payment to reach your account but we have found that the payment has usually gone in within a few days. This is very helpful to new operators as it provides good cash flow with regular payments coming in early on.

AirBnB is also generally better for hosts as they charge the least amount of commission. They have been very clever and split the cost of the booking between you and the guest where the guest pays around 8% service fee and you pay around the same. One downside is that there is no alternative method of payment with AirBnB, they require the guest to pay them and then they pay you. Other OTAs give you the option to take payments directly from the guest and then bill you the commission fee separately. However, as you generally receive the money within a few days of check-in, this doesn't affect operators significantly.

One other downside of AirBnB is that they also take payment of the security deposit and hold it on your behalf, making it very difficult to claim back anything that the guest has damaged during their stay. AirBnB do offer all hosts the security of $1,000,000 insurance per listing and say that they will pay for any damages that hosts incur as a result of an AirBnB guest. However, in practice this has proven to be quite different. If there are any disputes between guests and hosts, AirBnB will more often than not, side with the guest.

BOOKING.COM

Booking.com was initially set up for hotels who have dedicated staff and are familiar with hotel style invoicing and payments, so whilst it isn't the most user friendly to begin with, it's easy enough once you get the hang of it.

There are two methods of payment with Booking.com. Either they take the payment on your behalf and pay you monthly, or you take the payments directly. There are pros and cons to both, which we will explore.'

When you list your property, the default payment method is for Booking.com to take the payment on your behalf and pay you the monthly total minus the commission due. For example, let's say that for the whole month of August you get a total of £2,000 in bookings that have all checked out by 31st August, Booking.com will deduct their commission at 15% and pay you the £1,700 by 15th September. They tell you (similar to AirBnB) that the payment will be in your account by 15th of each month and in our experience, this has been the case with a couple of exceptions. This payment method can be very painful for new operators to use as you will need to make it through a month and a half without having any money from these bookings so if any maintenance issues crop up, you will need to pay for these some other way.

The main benefit of using this system is that Booking.com 100% guarantee the payment. So even if a guest has used a fraudulent card or disputes the payment after the stay, Booking.com will still pay you for the booking in full, even if they have had to issue a refund.

The alternative method of payment with Booking.com is where you take payments directly and then they issue an invoice for the commission for which you pay monthly. Booking.com provides you with the card details of the guest at the time of booking and you are required to take payment within 7 days, after which, they are hidden. Obviously, in order for you to take the payment you will need some type of card payment provider.

Booking.com also offer the option of you taking cash on arrival and for small operators or people operating meet 'n greet check-ins this may be preferable for some bookings, but this is obviously much riskier because if your guest doesn't turn up, then you have lost the booking and the money.

EXPEDIA

Expedia is much more complicated than any other OTA I have experienced. This was initially set up for Hotels exclusively and has now started adding individual properties on the website as an afterthought. The vast majority of Expedia's revenue still comes from Hotels so they don't have much of an incentive to put more effort into making their software more user friendly. Fundamentally, there are 2 methods of payment in Expedia: Hotel Collect and Expedia Collect.

Hotel Collect is where you, as the operator are responsible for collecting payment form the guest. This can either be done by taking cash on arrival or card payment. If you decide to do it via a card payment, then you will need to process that payment within 7 days of booking and also provide a receipt/invoice to the guest.

Expedia Collect, as you might expect, does what it says on the tin: Expedia takes payment on your behalf and pays you after the guest checks out. This is where it gets complicated though: Expedia Collect is itself split into 2 methods of payment: they either pay you directly into your account by the 15th of the following month for the previous months' bookings or they issue a virtual credit card (imaginatively called Expedia Virtual Card) for you to charge through your direct payment system. This virtual card has been known to be simply credit card details which you enter into your payment system or an actual Credit Card that they send you in the post pre-loaded with the credit of the stay which you can charge when it arrives in the post.

It has never been clear to me when you can expect either method of payment to be selected by Expedia. It possibly has something to do with the country the account is being charged from or the actual website that the booking is made through as Expedia listings show up on many other websites and therefore, may have different requirements for payment. If it sounds awfully complicated, it's because it is! So I suggest check each booking that comes through Expedia as to what you need to do to collect payment.

I have provided *Images 13* and *14* to show the different ways Expedia lets you know which method of payment has been selected and have circled what to look out for.

One other thing to mention is how Expedia collects its commission. They send you an invoice of the amount (15% of total bookings collected within the period) and collect via a Direct Debit or an invoice each month.

Just as a point of information, both Booking.com and Expedia put the payment dates on the 15th of the month for the bookings collected in the month prior to allow for any queries or disputes. So essentially, they give you 14 days to query or dispute the payments being made or requested, otherwise, you will be charged and paid the amounts stated. On Expedia, they have a section for this under 'Accounting' called 'Reconciliations' and with Booking.com they just ask you to contact the finance team directly through the Extranet for any queries of this nature, and they do generally get back to you within 24 hours.

Image 13

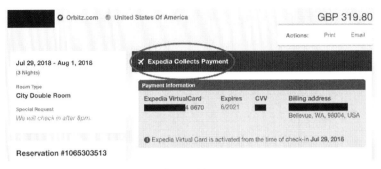

Image 14

DIRECT PAYMENTS

When taking payments directly, you will need some kind of card payment processor. This is simply a company that provides an online gateway that charges a card for you and forwards you the payment deducting the commission for the transaction. Just for clarity, we have never taken payments by cash, I personally feel that there is too much risk involved. I have heard many stories about guests being asked to pay in cash (usually for a last minute booking) and have told the host that they will leave the cash in an envelope when they leave. Of course, the envelope has mysteriously been lost or 'your cleaner must have taken it' leading to the host losing the money for the booking.

We use Stripe to process card payments but there are a few around for you to use such as WorldPay and Square, with the only real difference being the level of commission they charge per transaction. WorldPay are the market leaders and the processor of choice for all major retailers and big business. These are the majority of card machines that you see in retail shops and appear to be of the most benefit for businesses that take hundreds of transactions per day, but for small businesses just starting out then it becomes much more expensive.

Stripe are one of the cheapest and most established card processors for small businesses which is why we chose them. It's very easy to sign up with them and also to link the payment processor into other websites (such as your own) to provide instant payments when the guest books online.

It's important to keep in mind that whichever card payment processor you choose it should be able to link in easily with a website if you wish to create your own in the future.

YOUR FIRST GUESTS

When you have your listing up on the OTAs, in a high demand area, furnished to good specification, with some high quality images uploaded, your pricing set and calendars all linked together, your next step would be to get your first bookings. It's important to know that the different OTAs operate in different ways when it comes to reviews. Booking.com for example, require at least 5 reviews before they will list the average rating for your listing, whereas AirBnB and Expedia will show the number of reviews and average from the very first one you get.

I would recommend that you take any opportunities you have to go the extra mile for your guests on your initial bookings. We have in the past provided a bottle of Prosecco for our guests' 5-year wedding anniversary along with a note of congratulations, another time when a guest's son left their toy dog in our apartment, we got back in touch with the guest to ask for their address and sent them the toy back with a letter and some photos of the awesome adventure we'd taken he dog on during his time with us. Both times we received a 10/10 rating on Booking.com.

If you get the first 5 reviews averaging a 9/10, then the odd 5/10 will have a lot less weighting and affect your overall score much less. As always it's important to maintain standards as you continue to operate but it's crucial to get off to a good start.

MAINTENANCE ISSUES

It's inevitable that at some point during your SA operation you will encounter maintenance issues. It's very important to respond promptly to messages from guests regarding any issues that they encounter during their stay and even more important to dealt with everything quickly. We have had a variety of issues, from the electronic entry gate not opening due to a system failure to a guests' child locking themselves in the bathroom and not being able to get out.

The first thing you will need to consider is who exactly will fix these maintenance issues. Are you a handyman or handywoman? If you consider yourself one and would prefer to do these yourself, then you will need to be prepared to go to the property in the late evening or early hours to sort out these kinds of issues. We have managed to find a handyman who also lives in the building. We of course pay him for the time he takes to do these kinds of jobs as well as any materials that he needs. But this kind of relationship has been very useful to us as he is able to attend issues within minutes of us letting him know of the problem. This was particularly useful when the girl locked herself in the bathroom. Also, because we have 2 properties in the area, he's more than happy to go to the other apartment to sort any issues there. I have to say, if we didn't have this kind of arrangement, it would have cost us a lot more and we would have incurred many more negative reviews in the process. Without this kind of arrangement, you will need to find a 24Hr handyman and get their details. You will be able to find them on Facebook, Google, or 'TrustaTrader' but you may also find better quality recommendations from local letting agents or property managers as they use them all the time for their maintenance issues. Either way, it's absolutely vital that you find someone reliable to deal with these kinds of issues as it has serious implications to your guests' experience.

Here's the example of the electronic system failure mentioned earlier: It was around 11.00pm and it was pouring with rain where they were staying, the guest messaged me to tell me they couldn't get in. I asked them to make sure they were inputting the code correctly which they said they did.

'Yeah they always say that' I thought.

Then a video comes through of them inputting the code and nothing happening. Now what do I do? They are stuck out in the rain. I text our handyman, he's on holiday in North Wales. Now what? Do I drive down myself? Even if I did, what do I do when I get there? So I decided to call the 24Hr maintenance number of the building.

'Have you tried the other gate around the side of the building? We are aware of the issue but it's just that gate. Entry to the building from the side gate and to the building itself is working fine.' they told me. I relay this information back to the guest who managed to get back into the property fine. Panic over. This is a small example of some of the issues you'll need to be able to deal with and deal with at the time they occur. Especially issues with entry and exit to the property.

CANCELLATIONS

It is inevitable that at some point a guest will cancel on you. It's important not to get too disheartened when this happens as you just don't know other people's circumstances in life. What's more important, is that you protect your business properly by making it difficult for the guest to cancel at the last minute and that you minimise your losses. We operate a 30-day cancellation policy on all OTAs. This is where the guest can cancel and receive a full refund anytime up to 30-days prior to check-in date. After this period, they are charged the full value of the booking. There are obviously exceptions to this which are down to the specific functions of the OTA. For example, AirBnB operate a compulsory 48-hour grace period where the guest (or host) can cancel the booking within 48 hours without receiving a penalty.

Cancellations for the host are to be avoided as much as possible as they can be very costly. For example, with AirBnB if you haven't cancelled a booking within the past 6 months, then you will receive no penalty fees as they put this down to the fact that sometimes, things happen that cannot be avoided (essential urgent maintenance for example) and they let you off. If you cancel again though, they will start penalising you for it. Initially, they will charge a $100 cancellation fee and your listing will shoot down the results lists, and they go up from here. There is a compulsory review left on the listing with the cancellation and how many days prior to the reservation the cancellation occurred although it will not affect your star rating.

If the guest wishes to cancel during the stay because of essential maintenance or because they couldn't access the property adequately, then AirBnB will charge you a cancellation fee, then also charge you the cost of rehousing them in a 'similar' property at short notice. If your property is 10/10 rating, then this could easily be a 5-star hotel. So the host not only loses the booking fee and, receives a cancellation fee, the host is then charged for the guests' alternative accommodation in a similar property. I would say that the most common reason for a cancellation is a double booking due to calendars not being synched properly or the property management software (e.g. Tokeet) not automatically updating calendars.

Booking.com and Expedia policies on host cancellations are a little different and restrict the ability to cancel solely on the guest. Therefore, if you really need to cancel a reservation, you can ask the guest to cancel the reservation and usually, if you explain your predicament to the guest, they will cancel the reservation and go somewhere else. If you contact Booking.com and request to cancel through the extranet, they will want a very good reason why and if they accept and cancel the booking, they will still charge you a commission fee for the booking and occasionally block out your calendar so you cannot accept another booking. So it's obviously beneficial to avoid cancellations at all costs because some of those costs can be quite high. If you join a network of other operators, you might be able to pass a reservation off onto them without incurring any cancellation fees. As we haven't gone through this before, I'm unsure exactly how this works but I know people do this quite often when double-booked.

GUEST JOURNEY

As we're now getting towards the end of this book, I want to take you through the full guest journey with you so you have an idea for all the communications and interactions that occur from start to finish.

GUEST MAKES A BOOKING

The guest obviously starts by actually making a booking at some time in advance of their stay. As soon as a booking is made, we send a fully templated message with the confirmation and details of their stay attached, thanking them for their booking, letting them know that it's a self-check-in process and we will let them know the full details the morning of their check-in. We also offer to answer any questions they may have. Once this is sent we log onto 'YourWelcome' and input the guest details into the system as well as their email address and details of their stay.

THE MORNING OF CHECK-IN

If the guest asks any questions before the day of check-in, then we answer them as soon as it's convenient to do so. On the morning of the check-in, we let them know on the OTA messaging system that we will be sending them all the details of the check-in this morning to their registered phone number. In the same message we send them the full address just to make sure. Then, straight after, we text the guest with the following message:

Hi (Guest Name),

I will send you all the details of your upcoming stay in (City Name) now.

Just to confirm, the full address is (Full Street address of property).

This is the electronic entry to the building at the rear of the property, the code for this is XXXX.

(Video of me entering the code into the key pad)

Once inside the building please make your way to Apartment X (level X if using the lift) and in the doorway is the key box. The code for this is XXXX.

(Video of me opening the key box with the code).

Once inside please use the tablet on the kitchen counter to check-in.

There is complimentary Netflix with the apartment under profile 'Apartment X'

The Wi-Fi password for the property is - XXXXXXXXX

Let me know if you have any issues and I hope you enjoy your stay.

Many thanks

Ray

GUEST CHECK-IN

When the guest arrives at the property hopefully they won't have any issues with entry to the building and when they arrive in the kitchen, they will see the tablet displayed as 'Welcome (Guest). Please tap to check-in'.

They tap the screen then confirm their details and accept the terms and conditions with a tick box and confirm. After this, there is an initial survey asking for their initial rating of the property out of 5. Once they click submit this is sent to you along with the confirmation of the terms and conditions. This essentially lets you know if there are any immediate issues with the property. As a general rule, if the guest leaves anything under a 4/5 then get in touch with them and ask if there's anything wrong.

We have contacted guests who have clicked the wrong number but other times the cleaner has left a few hairs in the sink and the guest was not too impressed. Either way though, it gives you an idea of what the guest thinks of the property before they give you a rating on the OTA.

THE MORNING OF CHECK-OUT

On the morning of the day that the guests are due to check-out, we will send the following text:

Hi (Guest Name),
You are due to check-out this morning at 10.00am. I hope you have enjoyed your stay at (Name of Apartment building)

please check-out using the tablet on the kitchen counter, lock the front door and leave the key in the key box when you leave.

Many thanks and have a safe journey.

Ray

GUEST CHECK-OUT

At around 8.00am the tablet in the kitchen displays the following message:

'Your check-out time is 10:00am. Tap to check-out now.'

The guest taps the screen and is given a check-out survey to fill out which is simply:

'How would you rate your stay?'   /5

'Would you recommend your stay to others?'   Yes/No

This is again sent to you via email and is a good indicator what your official review on the OTA will be.

HORROR STORIES

For the final part of this book, I thought it would be good to finish with some short but absolute horror stories of hosts experiences. All stories below are absolutely true and have happened to other hosts. Thankfully, we haven't had such experiences yet (touch wood), but I still find great benefit from these and I am grateful these hosts tell their stories so that others know what to watch out for and what to do if such a thing ever happens.

REALLY?

Guest books American hosts apartment through Expedia with a $500 security deposit. Stays in the apartment and caused damage to the property (nothing too major) and lost the set of keys. Host gets in touch with Expedia showing pictures of before and after guest stay, letter from cleaner detailing damage on arrival and loss of keys. Guests admit via text to causing the damage.

Host gets damage repaired, issues penalty fee for replacement set of keys and sends invoices for extra cleaning required. Altogether came to $600. Host charges guests card $600 through Expedia. Guest contacts bank and disputes the transaction. After a brief exchange between host and guests' bank, they are assured that as they've admitted damage, dispute is overwhelmingly likely to be very straight forward and ruled in hosts favour.

Dispute ends in guests' favour.

Host gets in touch with Expedia who explain that as it's the guests bank that has issued the result this has nothing to do with Expedia and unfortunately, there is nothing they can do for the host.

Really? Yep.

EVERY HOST'S WORST NIGHTMARE

AirBnB guest books last minute at 6pm for 11pm check-in and a 2-night stay. Host was a little concerned because his profile had no picture or reviews but was happy to get the booking in.

Two days later host gets a call from the cleaner saying they better come down to the property as there's a problem. Host goes to the property to find that their worst nightmare has materialised. It has to fall on someone and this time it was him. His guest has absolutely trashed the place. £150 rug burned. £400 HD TV keyed. Chairs through walls. Strong smell of marijuana. White powder on tables. Laughing gas canisters on the floor. Bedding everywhere and cut to shreds. Fire extinguisher sprayed all over the kitchen. Bottles all over the place. Empty pizza boxes all over the floor. Glass coffee table smashed.

It happened. What people warned him about taking random guests happened, what he only heard happened to other people happened to him.

He got in touch with AirBnB who wanted pictures and invoices for everything to claim under their hosts insurance but only to make the claim after 72 hours. Three days go by, the host collects all the evidence and invoices for repairs and sends them to AirBnB to make a claim. AirBnB reply to say that you can only claim within 48 hours of check-out so they are unable to help.

EVEN THE FURNITURE?

Guest books apartment through Booking.com who take payment for the host. Host asks for ID and for guest to sign T&C's to which they happily provide a National Identity Card and agree to the T&C's.

The morning of the guest check-out the hosts cleaner rings to ask if she decided to remove the TV and some furniture. She hadn't. The guest hadn't spent their time in the apartment relaxing and enjoying the place, but loading up the TV and living room furniture into a van with a few friends to take home with them.

Host contacts Booking.com who explain that as she did not take a deposit there's nothing for her to claim against. Host calls police and gives them the picture of the National Identity Card the guest provided. Police say they can only help with Passports because National ID Cards are easily forged. Booking.com guarantee the payment so at least the reservation is still paid for. Just not the living room furniture or the TV.

A FINAL NOTE

From a serviced accommodation enthusiast to another, I want to thank you for purchasing this book. If I have managed to answer one question or help you in any way, then this book has achieved its purpose. The last piece of advice I want to leave you with is: have a go! Research is not an excuse for not taking action and you'll learn more from doing it yourself than reading any number of books. Good luck!

For access to the free download of the Resources for this book, visit our Facebook page for Insight Serviced Apartments.

Printed in Great Britain
by Amazon